WOMAN IN THE TREES

WOMAN IN THE TREES

Poems on Climate and Nature

SAMI RAFIQ

Hawakal
PUBLISHERS
New Delhi | Calcutta

HAWAKAL PUBLISHERS PRIVATE LIMITED
70 B/9 Amritpuri, East of Kailash, New Delhi 65
33/1/2 K B Sarani, Mall Road, Calcutta 80

Email info@hawakal.com
Website www.hawakal.com

Cover designed by Bitan Chakraborty

First edition (paperback) November 2022

ISBN: 978-93-91431-79-2 (paperback)

Price: INR 350 | USD 14.99

for
Asim, my husband
and
Kaif and Kainaat

FOREWORD

It is a truism to say that we live in a period of climate emergency, despite the ignorance preferred by many governments, and people hardly do anything about it. Limited government action, including the Indian Government, is inconspicuous. Despite having national governments, we are subjected to arguably the biggest global issue we have ever faced. The wilful destruction of nature is a form of international suicide that comprehensively affects plants, animals, and humans. Sami Rafiq's *Woman in the Trees* is a poetic response to this crisis. The collection functions as a poetry of protest but also concerns empathy with nature, memory, and the apprehensive nature of humans relating to the time.

It is reasonable to ask, 'What is the point of poetry at this time?' W. H. Auden said, 'Poetry makes nothing happen!' But against this, we must set Aristotle's declaration in his *Poetics*, 'Poetry is something more philosophical and more worthy of serious attention than history.' Poetry speaks to the deepest part of ourselves, our psyches, or what is still occasionally called 'the soul'. If our outward political action is devoid of something, then it must be our most intense inward selves that might desire to make leaders initiate change.

In attempting to do so, Sami Rafiq joins a long poetic effort stretching back to the Romantics—in poetry and the other arts. Poetry has always attended and drawn from nature, which is not human-made and therefore lies outside our egos. It lives and provides the context for all our lives. Wordsworth, Coleridge, and the other English Romantic poets are now often read in reference to ecological context; they refuted the previous era's conception of the world. They discarded the notion of the world as a brilliant machine set in motion by God and instead likened the world to a plant. This is the origin of the contemporary idea of 'the living planet', an idea that renders the thematic linearity of the poems in *Woman in the Trees.*

Sami Rafiq's poems encompass a wide range of flowers, vegetables, fruits, and animals, as well as human situations, reflecting an intrinsic interaction between them. She pays particular attention to trees because of their importance to her childhood.

My green friend—
Casket of carvings and yearnings;
How does a tree hold on
To past, present, and future?

—My Green Friend

A tree can be a 'green friend' partly because it holds on 'To past present, and future', clenching the sky above its head and the earth under its feet. Trees have an 'ageless wisdom', which she knew back in her childhood and now rediscovers once again. 'New trees are sacred letters' akin to what Coleridge viewed nature as, God's language in a different climate in *Frost at Midnight.*

Her poetry argues that we are 'nature's guests'. Together, with her direct concern of nature's destruction comes an intense interest in the past 'old seasons long gone', as it relates to the present, with the connections between childhood and adulthood, with the psychology of dreams and the unconscious versus the conscious mind. The past will 'awaken somewhere' in the unconscious mind, and many routes will reveal the importance of poetry to the human spirit and evoke awareness concerning nature. 'Pain' is a 'dreamer', and Rafiq's poems implicitly point to the dangers of human activity if acted alone.

Dennis Haskell, AM
Poet, Emeritus Professor,
The University of Western Australia

Introduction

I would like to, at the onset, justify the title *Woman in the Trees*. I see my mother amidst the trees, and then I see myself—amidst the trees. But more than that, I see the poorest women working in tea gardens and crop fields, closely associated with nature and her seasons for a livelihood. Nature and trees are their lifelines. Demolition of the same would ruin their lives—hence the title *Woman in the Trees.*

I have spent most of my life since childhood until now amid poetry and trees. When I was studying in Nainital, nature was a close ally—all her moods mine, and mine hers. I observed the torrential rains in the hills and the numerous insects with the change of seasons such as caterpillars, leeches, and slugs. I watched the sunny green hills reflecting the lights or walked through the lush wet pine forest on Saturday evenings—these experiences were functional in shaping my life. The chilblains, the biting winds, and the first frost did not hurt so much; in turn it gave me an emotional companionship.

My secondary schooling in Gwalior in Madhya Pradesh, too, was midst nature's plenty. Nature provided me with a change of aspect in the plains, with long sunny summers, close encounters with the ceremonial fruit, the sacred banana tree, and the banyan tree with its thousand roots.

My late father, Rafiq Pilibhiti, was a poet who wrote in Urdu. He gave me the first notes of the music of verse. The poem *Parinde ki faryad* by Iqbal stirred something deep in my soul and was about a bird that lost its nest in the gardens. My father's verse hovers like a breeze around me till today.

Rafiq aankhein nahin khulti hain meri in shuaaon mein
Ujaalon se kaho todein hijab ahista ahista

(Rafiq I am unable to open my eyes to this brilliance
Tell the lights to lift the veil slowly)

My mother, a lover of literature, is also a lover of flowers and trees. Together they initiated me into the world of trees and poetry. I remember the huge garden in my parents' house in Amir Nishan, Aligarh—filled with guava, neem, peach, eucalyptus, lemon, and custard apple trees. There was something magical about the trees. I felt it in my heart but could never put my finger on the pulse. I remember studying under those trees, especially the poems of Keats and Wordsworth. When the house was sold and turned into a flat, I felt something crash within me. I reconfigured my loss as the loss of the bird in Iqbal's poem. I felt like the proverbial bird that lost its garden forever:

Jab se chaman chuta hai yeh haal ho gaya hai
Dil gham ko kha raha hai, gham dil ko kha raha hai
Gaana ise samajh ke khush ho na sunne wale
Dukhe hue dilon ki fariyad ye sadah hai.

—Allama Iqbal

(Ever since I lost my garden, this is my state
The heart lives on grief and grief lives on the heart
Readers should not take this as a happy song
This song is the plea of sorrowing hearts.)

For me, it was not just the loss of a paradise but a loss of the habitat of numerous birds, insects, and animals that dwelt there for over thirty years. For almost three decades, in this sanctuary of nature that was our house, I learned to appreciate the seasons of spring, summer, monsoon, and winter. The doves and the sparrows had the same nesting places over the years, and we had watched the cycle of eggs, hatchlings, and empty nests close up. My father's gentle verses lent their emotion to those vegetables in the winter garden, those purple brinjals, those dill leaves that were dear to me, those peppy tomatoes and cauliflowers, and so forth. It is only now, when I reimagine my mother under those trees, the waving field of red poppies and calendula, like a figure in a painting by Manet, that I begin to refigure those shaping influences in my life.

Hoards of butterflies, bees, wasps, hummingbirds, sparrows, crows, nightingales, and doves would be all over the place. When I see less of them now, it saddens me. I have realized that after teaching poetry and literature for over twenty-five years. Now, nothing purports my deep connection with nature. However, the wreckage and obliteration of trees, and long concrete roads without shade, have made me turn to poetry for solace. Yes, the trees bring comfort when I close my eyes. Perhaps, I feel that writing about them and nature would bring them comfort too.

This volume of verse on climate change and the environment focuses on several issues: emotional, environmental, domestic, or political. Some of the poems employ words and phrases from different languages. Since nature is the matrix of human concerns therefore, they are all indirectly linked to climate change and the environment. The poems also promote human values and global unity and attempt to foster sensitivity towards trees, animals, plants, and other non-human entities to undo the effects of climate change and restore harmony and promote unity on the planet.

This collection of poems is a prayer for love, peace, and harmony.

Sami Rafiq
Aligarh Muslim University

Contents

Butterfly Diary

Holding the butterflies made my fingers
slippery with their pollen;
Strange how the past and the present seemed to merge
into each other like designs on butterfly wings.
I remember in my childhood,
chasing those butterflies across the fields,
Bringing them back in a fist,
or in a pinch holding the wings,
Which were green or spotted black or butter yellow.
Catching those butterflies was like visualizing
a strange collection of dreams;
And then when the butterflies were put into a cage,
I saw the damaged rings,
And the bodies creeping along
with their giant, innocent, helpless feelers,
Like lost creatures from another universe.

Then in childhood reveries, I mixed all those colors of dreams
together and made a butterfly paste out of them—
It never occurred to me how unthinkably cruel
it was to even unconsciously imitate a shrinking universe,
where the collapsed mass would create new stars.

It is the same self today, that abhors
the butterfly collectors' prize collections,
Where butterfly specimens are pinned in place.

Falling Tree

There was a storm last night,
Heavy rain and lightning too,
The old tree that had stood years
Outside,
Collapsed with a sigh—
He was my image,
My replica,
Only I could feel his pain.
When I arched brokenly
There was no sound at all—
Of cracking or creaking,
No sound at all;
Except for the jabbing dagger of light,
That had been inching close,
Unable to strike me down.
But now it struck me in the heart!
The fall itself was slow,
A slow and steady bending,
As if under a burden,
Till all the sinews
Gave way and crumbled.
Methinks there was no one there at all—
Who could see a tree;
Who could hear it crash to the ground;
There was someone there—
Who saw the birds and nests,
And cried—
At the falling of a tree.

Rose

Ensconced in her veils,
A fuchsia smile;
Perfumed like a bride,
She sits unseen,
Bedecked and concealed;
Camouflaged in pink eddies,
Till the fiery sun,
Unravels her sacred selves.

Of her many curved petals,
The honey bee was drunken
In overwhelming fascination;
Lying motionless,
On the ground beneath her veils.

Her face turns deep crimson,
As she continues her discourse
With elements in the air—
And the breeze whispers.

The rain pelts her,
Tapping each petal;
Rain-soaked,
Dew soaked,
Heavy with anguish—
Like one having wept all night.

Woman in the Trees

She awaits dawn,
To dry her tears;
Once more rough winds,
Like ruthless hoards,
Attempt to tear her up—
Again, she resists.

Her flawless demeanor,
Reflects her beloved's face;
She pulls her shawls closer,
But the cold hits home—
Entropy prevails.

Midst disintegrating portieres,
Out of seventy thousand veils,
Only a few remain—
Revealing her beloved's face.

The day brightens,
The storm dies;
Slowly she lowers,
Her once lovely head—
The moment
Was chosen for her.

Hydrangeas

Blue, pink, yellow,
the Hydrangeas—
Come to me in dreams;
With their heavenly touch,
Against my cheeks.
Old seasons long gone,
Awaken somewhere;
When the hills were green,
And dirt tracks
Redolent of horse droppings,
Seemed never-ending.
Our slow ponies,
Trotted in uniform motion,
Encircling a teeming lake,
Full of myths and folk tales;
Conversing with mad yachts,
Arching like dying moths,
On the silvery waters,
In the pale breeze.
But in dream, worlds submerge
Into wakefulness—
Yesterday the pony track,
Collapsed into the lake,
Killed by rain, feet,
And tires!
Cars like grave beetles,
Drone a death knell,
To the Hydrangeas,
And the green hills.

Baying Dogs

No sounds in the dark!
Even crickets are quiet tonight!
But suddenly—
The mournful baying,
Rises like a crescendo.
Over our stillness,
The moon hangs low,
Gloomily watching,
The sound touches trees,
The earth shakes,
With the tumultuous,
Long drawn wails!
Narrating histories,
The sound sweeps,
Through the leaves!
Tears the grass,
Rides on the wind;
One howl multiplying,
As if on Twitter or Facebook!
Across an invisible network,
They know their words,
The highs and lows,
Reflecting on the rise and fall—
Of tides,
Of rivers,
Of forests,
They know like ancient natives—

That the scourge of man
Is coming!
Not like old times with arrows,
But with deathly media networks,
The 4G,
The 5G,
The Alexa detonators!
The gleaming razor fangs of radiation,
Of online pleasure seeking!
They are baying—
The cry of despair,
The loss of worlds.
They mourn—
The oncoming Demolition!

Expressionist Canvas

A river—
Cutting estuaries,
Flooding pebbles and grime;
At times through echoes,
Crossing a lonely shell,
In
spiralling columella.
Traveling seasons—
Of numbness and burns,
Embroidering thorny hedges,
Painting cobbled pathways,
Seeping blood into dry soils,
Heavy with dead sighs,
Reminder of bone longings;
Pain the Dreamer—
Casts about
A fishing net,
Full of sea splinters,
And salt water.

My Mother

My Mother,
A wilting spring,
Sleeps—
Off and on;
In her bouquet,
Of a white bed.
Its been long,
Since she was clipped,
From my father;
Who took off alone—
His wings her sky,
Her days and nights,
Her storms and spoils.
Ever since he went,
On his way,
To the stars—
She's a grey spot
In a make-believe painting.
One who lived,
Splashing color long ago—
Smiling scarlet dahlias,
Painting green guava leaves,
Watering tender pink lilies.
Our bedsheets—
Were her masterpieces.
My mother—
That unhappy flower,
Now out of season,
Looks at me,
In monochrome!

The Peace of Birds

The showy green pheasant is singing,
Daiski dis, daiski dis, daiski dis,
Putting his love in Japanese,
And though he is game,
For others' meat,
He swears by peace.
The falcon in Arabia al Saqr,
Who preys on smaller birds?
But will not feed beyond his hunger,
Sings poised high in the sky,
Aana Mamnoon, Aana mamnoon, Aana mamnoon,
I am grateful for every blessing and every boon;
Jeeshoo the buzzard from the native Indian camp,
Came alive and began to sing—
Hodeezyeel!
Hodeezyeel!
Hodeezyeel!
Harmony! Harmony! Harmony!
Erase the memory of past agony;
The humble rooster from a farm,
Became France's symbol,
Of self and sexuality,
Yet it cries in French—
Je suis humble, je suis humble, je suis humble,
Je chante pour la paix,
Paix, Paix, Paix.
Peace, peace, peace.

The majestic golden eagle of Scotland,
Seeks refuge from human violence,
Calls deep from the Keatsian Hebrides,
Itealaich combla rium sgiathan na sithe!
Fly with me on the wings of peace—
Trocaire!
Trocaire!
Trocaire!
Mercy,
Mercy,
Mercy.

The sweet-throated nightingale,
Has sung through centuries in Iran,
Man dar rahe sulah hastam!
Man dar rahe sulah hastam!
Man dar rahe sulah hastam!
Even the haughty peacock,
Joined the songs for peace,
Singing for India—
Prem mera dharm hai,
Main prem ki dhanak hoon,
Prem!
Prem!
Prem!
The pheasant's joined in again,
Tomadachi ga atsumatte!
Friends let's come together!
Mohabbat hamari manzil hai
Hum prem ke rahi hain!

Neem

Your branches—
Lower to my aspirations,
And blossom my buried desires;
The shape of your leaves,
Your intense bitterness,
The outcome of my illusions!
Neem—-
My rooted blossom,
In once-polluted soils.

My time-worn heart—
Has learned to recycle
Sadness, desperation, rejections;
All to a bitter salve,
For blisters on our souls,
For you and me;
There's always the axe—
Of worldly profits!

One day
When I
Retire,
Tired—
To our soil bed;
And you stand alone,
To face

The unseen ones;
I pray
Their offspring
The berries of my soul—
May breathe their bitterness
Into poisoned sweetness!

Saawan

Come rain,
Come today,
Come lift the heat;
The rainbird cries,
Through waves of heat,
But still, the air is choked.
Frog rhythm lies buried;
Just one raindrop trickles down,
Along a leaf,
Across a pane,
Down my cheek,
The song of parting plays;
The rain doesn't pour!
A haughty peacock in fading colors,
Looks up midst plastic wrappers,
And fuming swirls of petroleum;
Come rain,
Come today,
Come lift the heat.

Perth: Images

Swan river—
The dream of Nyoongars,
Slowly drifts,
In memories;
A cache—
Of sea birds,
And peacocks,
Freshwater turtles,
Slowly,
Shadowing,
Human feasts;
The eerie calls,
Of magpies,
And ravens,
Shuffling,
Though forgotten;
Wagyl—
The rainbow serpent still lurks,
In the sacred land,
Hungering,
To fold the Swan River,
In its giant coils.

Bangles

The bangles—
You and I dreamt of,
In sunset colors,
In ocean blues,
Ripened wheat fields,
Dying landscapes;
Are they,
death knells?
toxic truths?
chimney smoke?
Ashen rivers of vomit,
from sick, emaciated landscapes?
Birthings of the bangles,
Where fires are lit,
Burning fingers deliver,
Burning hearts give shape,
Life surrenders its blood and colors,
For the bride's sacred wrist!
Around a ceremonial fire,
On a European catwalk,
And no one will check—
The fevers and the fires
That still flickers,
In the trending bangles!

Yellow

The yellow,
Flashes upon the inward eye,
When Poonam,
Poured the pineapple slices,
From the can,
Into her sister's plate;
The sunshine pineapple tints,
Dazzled the senses,
Leaving a heady sweetness;
I can still see her,
In her pretty pinafore,
Bending over her little sister,
Pouring yellow sunshine,
Onto a plate.

Where is that yellow today?
Only grim pineapple heads,
Buried in flower pots!
Wretched and cursed like humans—
Living in digital worlds!

Fake soil!
Fake oxygen!
Fake water!
I look at my empty plate,
Drizzled with darkness,
And wish,
For a dollop of sunshine!

Paradise Lost

Another morning,
Of light and song;
Another morning,
Of heavenly grace;
Yet another morning,
Where eyes awaken,
To wings and colors;
Another morning,
Of diamonds and rubies,
In emerald earth;
Another morning,
Of thanks for health;
Another morning,
To look into the mirror,
To see the eyes,
To see the skin,
To feel the breath;
Another morning,
To see the beauty of her face,
Reflections of scars and cracks;
Another morning,
All beauty all grace,
Midst all this beauty;
Why must humans,
Be a crooked, sinking scar,
In her deserts,

In her tears,
In her breaths?
Another morning now—
The ashes of her rubies and diamonds,
Blot out,
The heavenly sky.

My Green Friend

The moment I lift my eyes,
You appear like a ghost—
Dim sparkler
Against a grey sky;
When heaven's light
Peeps through a crack;
In the solemn skies,
My green friend—
An amazing burst of leaves,
An explosion of grey, gold, green,
Before my surprised glance.
My green friend—
Casket of carvings and yearnings;
How does a tree hold on
To past, present, and future?
To be so firmly rooted,
In tumultuous tempo!
In grains of galaxies!
Having traveled with me,
Through ageless eons—
My friend, my air;
My friend, my matrix;
My friend, my canvas;
My friend, my pen;
My friend, my thoughts;
Liquid, solid, gas,
No wonder—
This flash of recognition,
The gentle touch of a friend,
On my weary shoulder.

A Conversation

Like a human hand,
The Young Spruce,
Extends a branch,
Leafy fingers,
Outstretched,
Poised in air,
What levitation is this?
What remarkable balance?
With no muscles and bones?
What engaging felicity?
With sun air and grass,
All on the side,
Of a busy road;
In a dense grotto,
My Neem tree friends,
You are everywhere;
In darkness and light,
In
blue, grey, and green,
Sky, Earth, Hill, Plain,
Till death do us part—
In Heaven, Hell and Purgatory.
My friends, you are legends—
Hercules and Naushirwaan,
Fighting machines and robots!
What means it to be a tree?
To be old gnarled and timeless?

To hold the sky on your head?
To balance the earth under your feet?
What arms, what sinews, what tissues,
Blood, sweat, rain running warm,
Nurturing new generations;
While our blood turns cold,
With cash and comfort,
We are the Biblical and Quranic dead,
Deaf to unseen sleepers,
Deep in the earth,
Whose precious visions,
Mock our ignorance!

When I first spoke to a tree,
It was a silly thing;
For trees have neither eyes,
Nor ears,
Nor tongue.
The Banyan was nothing but swings,
The Neem was nothing but bitterness,
The Teak was nothing but wood,
Till my first meeting
With the trees;
Not really the first,
I always told my sadness,
To the jamuns, oaks, banyans, and neems;
Their silence always brought solace.
When I was young—
The branches were hands,
The flowers were eyes,
The fruits were faces;
I used to think,
When I was young,
When I talked to a tree
It heard me,

But could not talk back;
Everyone called it gibberish!
But now the trees,
Share their ageless wisdom,
My wish, my greeting, my touch,
Sets the network moving—
Sugars and salts of benevolence,
Work their chemistry on me.
Histories of times past sweep,
Coursing along an invisible line,
Trickling to younger trees.
My friend—
The Pine tree whispers,
Teaching me salvation,
To seek the heights,
Of blissful forgetfulness.

Memories

Imagine a turtle,
Candle on its back,
Flickering,
Through darkness;
Brown and white pigeons,
Feeding their young;
Rolling cotton clouds of rabbits,
Along a grey turf;
Chickens, parrots, a bulbul,
All in tremulous cadence;
Celebrating life and living,
My shoes are muddy,
The wind is in my face,
I cross over the furrows,
Encircling pools of water,
The goat kid skips after me,
The cows and buffaloes,
Eye me sympathetically,
The speckled goat,
Drinks tea on her knees,
A terminally ill dog,
Lives many golden years,
Such a scrapbook,
Is my childhood;
Open it where I will,
Pasted—
With dog-eared pictures,
Feathery silhouettes,
Dogs' faces that are human,
Human faces are dim.

Modern Love

She just couldn't say,
Love me forever—
The road,
Was looping far away,
The potholes, one too many;
She wished she could say,
Love me forever—
But the vehicle was too shaky,
To hold even the coffee cup straight,
How could anyone hold love forever,
When it trembled like a coffee cup,
And grew cold in seconds;
She wished she could say
Love me forever—
But the dust got into her eyes,
The contacts drew tears,
All she saw was a pastiche,
Choking, fading wearing, breaking,
Veils and shadows,
She wished she could say,
Love me forever—
But road rage swelled,
Snarled and held up traffic,
Cheating hawkers and sellers,
Made a hole in the pocket,
Too much to cope unaided,
So she reached out for the pills,

Placebos, tranquilizers, antidepressants;
Before she uttered the golden words,
To her silent companion,
The Chemist handed her a long bill,
Yet she must say them somehow,
Those words that just escaped her mind,
Yet heart and tongue twisted,
Groping along alleys of time and tense,
Along with sugar-free and long walks;
She tried to mumble those lines,
Like a new actor on a stage,
She stammers, stutters, stumbles,
And the blinding fresnels,
Give her the shape,
Of a burning meteor,
In quick descent.

Trees

You—
My Knights in shining armor,
Like Buddha's *Bodhi Tree*,
My mango tree;
Where I read the *Kabbalah*,
Learned how the letters,
Appear and disappear in a text;
With the passage of time,
New trees are sacred letters,
Scripted by the holy hand,
Bringing unseen sustenance—
Through fire, breath, blossom and fruit,
Through roots, through stems, through saps,
How could I possibly survive without you!
Your death augurs disaster,
Defiling of a sacred script.

The ancient tribes long ago,
Their praise and worship lost!
Protection of mighty beings,
No longer needed;
Today how shall a mountain stand,
Without the crowning headband?
Who will hold the restless of the earth?
Who will tie up the rivers,
Like silver braids,
And stop the eyes from turning,

Into tears…

My Knights in shining armor,
I saw your ghostly forms,
In the barren hills,
And in the desert where lilies bloomed!

A while ago.

Romeo Rooster

His origins:
The wicker basket of a worn biker,
A seller of farm chickens;
When old enough,
He lived with his harem,
Of plump brown hens;
There seemed nothing special,
About a homegrown rooster,
Who crowed,
At all the odd hours;
But his mad caroling,
Had a history of loss,
And joy and loss again.

Romeo lost his wives many times,
And survived their deaths each time,
And older and wiser was he,
With each one's passing;
But we were the targets,
Of his rage at fate's unfair deals,
He came at us like a missile,
We scrambled for safety,
Each time grateful for the netting;
We thought to cool his anger,
By procuring some more wives;
It worked like a charm—
Romeo had his fawning Juliets,

Romeo was so caring and so kind,
Guarding them ever,
From our evil intentions;
When tragedy struck again,
And again!
Each time outlived the scourge,
Or survived the cat's fangs,
The last time,
We saw him sit,
Unhappy, drooping, broken,
In the corner of the yard;
"Looks suicidal," the children remarked.
This made us pick up speed,
To get a new family,
Romeo sprang to life,
With his new family,
Once again—
He was an inspiration to forget pain,
To love, love and love again.

Harpy the Hawk

Before Harpy came along,
I always saw hunting birds,
As menacing evil raptors,
With cruel vicious claws;
But Harpy reminded me,
Of how cruel humans are;
One day,
I found in a heap,
Baby Harpy Hawk,
With maybe a broken wing,
Or an injured leg,
But the truth was sadder.

He had a string,
Tied to his leg,
Cutting his skin and sense,
A sign of brutal boy games.

With fear and trepidation,
I ventured near the hawk,
The sight of the huge talons,
And the curved yellow beak,
Took my breath away.

How wrong was I,
As I later learnt—
He was gentler than a child!

Perching on the highest point in my garden,
He surveyed the world below,
All the vanities and deceptions,
All the darkness and brightness,
Of lives that passed him by,
Were captured in his shiny eyes.

Nothing ever escaped him,
Neither men nor mice nor gnats,
He was a burning flame of fury,
To intruders—
But for us,
He lowered his proud head,
For a caress.

He grew in beauty,
Tranquility and poise;
When he glided away,
Sage like—
To other realms,
Unknown to us;
I realized,
The mythic hawk,
Was a visitation,
Of wisdom and love,
From other dimensions.

Dow Jones

Long ago—
When we came to earth,
We were nature's guests,
Our host laid out before us,
Bounties innumerable—
The shelters were countless,
Her foods were numberless,
Her moods were untamed;
The Goddess—
Taught us of abundance,
Of love and adoration,
And the patterns of harmony.

We learned about birth from her,
Love, death, decay, and rebirth,
Music from the birds, leaves, and rivers,
Art from the sunsets, trees, and mountains,
Indebtedness to the ocean, seas, rain, and winds;
How is it today—
We hear no music anymore,
We see no art anymore,
We seek no mystery anymore,
No more do we wonder and worship,
The good God who made them all—
Is nowhere to be found.
We go about our daily lives,
Like fractured ruined creatures,
Counting, totaling, charting,
Incurring losses—
That even Dow Jones cannot average!

Thorns

The thorns of the rose,
That draws blood;
The winter wind,
That makes teeth chatter;
The midsummer sun,
That wilts flowers,
And the skin;
All in Shakespeare's words—
Are not so harsh or cruel,
Like the human mind and tongue,
That dissembles, defeats, demolishes!
Nature's harshness is for all,
In floods, storms, and quakes—
Nature's fury is unabated,
Methinks its a hidden rage,
Against thankless humans,
Who try to wipe her out!

Bird on a Pole Tip

Mid winter's mild sun,
Against a haze of clouds,
The shadow of a hawk,
Perched single on a pole.
Var kommer du—
Are you a Swedish black hawk,
Waiting to be filmed?
What was the last recall,
In your reclusive mind?
Are you all alone?
Or just a dot,
Obstructing channels in the sky?
What language do you speak?
Is it eloquent or opulent?
What has caused you to halt
On the tip of a pole?
What is your creed,
That you sit mindful and insensate
Amidst—
The cacophony near you?

Sun

A spiraling Van Gogh sun,
In a brushed Van Gogh sky,
Grass scrawled in crooked script,
Das ist Van-Gogh Welt.

Uneven flights of fancy,
Inky birds on a wire,
A rare crow scrambling out,
Midst careless raining gunshots,
Das ist Van-Gogh Welt.

Deep dark quivering blots,
Of Van Gogh trees,
Bleeding refulgent colors,
Of spring, summer, and song,
Das ist Van-Gogh Welt.

The Van-Gogh heart,
Today throbs everywhere,
In autumn profusion;
No pastels—
No pink or blue or green,
Only rust, browns, blacks,
A lost Van Gogh Universe,
Das ist nicht die Van-Gogh Welt.

The Glider

How gracefully she glides,
On a straight course,
In perfect balance.
She taught the aircraft,
The art of flying!
Against a sunless sky,
She sails before my eye,
What must be the goal,
Of her steel gaze?
She stalks in the air,
Her unsuspecting prey,
In a clean-powered game.
How unmindful is she,
Of what goes on below,
In the name of living,
Uneven shanties!
Competing flats!
Road frenzy!
Hawkers homeless on sidewalks!
Sunless lives,
All small intrusions to,
Her motionless wings,
In her grand flight upward,
With the kill in her claws.

Weeds

We Indians,
Are really indifferent,
To weeds on balconies,
Or on slimy cobblestones,
They spring up everywhere,
Spreading out chicken legs,
From carcasses and severed,
dead fowls rotting on streets.
Unwelcome guests,
These weeds in Indian homes,
Overstay their stolen time;
They mind not—
Storms, rains, summer suns,
In floods, clouds, and wind;
They stay rooted,
Like lovers in memories.
Should someone decide,
They ought to go,
With a persistent,
Rant of destruction,
And a show of loathing,
They like slow-abiding elders,
Give one a gentle nod,
Of incomprehension,
And go on flowering.

Virtual Winters

Waking and sleeping,
No more with ellipses,
Up on a rumpled bed,
Breakfast rolled into dinner,
A sleepless, sleepwalker,
Logged online.

A teacher's unfamiliar voice,
Her quick combed hair,
Her sepia persona,
Her punctured voice,
All creeping in,
Slowly, indistinguishably.

Her voice—
A harmless droning,
An empty buzzing,
On inmates in a prison,
All we know of her,
Is her insistent gnawing,
Of our sleep-drowned pillow.

Who will tell her,
Of our private hells,
Closed in by manga,
And online thrills,
Frozen Covid winters,

Wilting mutated springs,
Dementia and deaths,
We do not know,
Where we are?

Her Covid scarred eyes,
Railing at work not done,
We know nothing of her trail,
Her tattered soul,
Stitched to each lesson,
Her grinding rituals,
Of measuring—
Seasons, deaths, lives,
In steaming teacups.

Do we even know each other,
Virtually reluctant time travelers,
Neither of us know mortality,
We are here forever,
Behind a silent screen,
Our endless cosmos is hate,
We scratch, tap, click, itch,
Like restless cats on heat.

Carpenter Bee/The Lunatic

On the grey terrace,
Lies a Carpenter bee,
A black shiny round spot,
How many seconds did he live?
Dancing among the flowers,
Exulting in the poisoned juices,
Tasting of steel, metal, gunpowder,
So unlike the honey of dreams.

In his dreams—
Bhawra was the lunatic,
Gyrating around his beloved,
His eyes feasted on her petals,
His soul bathing in her perfume,
His voice buzzing with love's tune,
His flight made him a pilgrim
Drunk with her beauty.

She offered him nectar,
Of splintered plastic hearts,
Mangled domains of media,
Carbons in cold morning dew,
Dust of long lost loves,
Smiling from moldy
pics,
The poison singed his wings.

And yet he danced,
His charred wings,
Churning a choir,
He was no more a bee,
But a ray and a gleam,
A pale fading dot,
On the firmament.

Light

I once saw a light,
In dreams,
And held its rays,
Till morning,
Carrying it to the cobbled path.

Now and then,
I look for that vagrant light,
In eyes, in smiles, in strange faces,
In gazes of wonder and bewilderment.

Sometimes a smile betrays,
Full of brightness and hope,
I rejoice in having found,
The light I borrowed,
Then I swear never to lose it again.

But once again,
Darknesses overcome,
Every gleaming iota,
The light is a mere shadow,
A mere reflection.

Once more I start to search,
For a small ray of light,
In the setting sun at dusk,
In the stars at night,
In the streaks of dawn,
Why is it that we dream,
Only once.

The Intruder

A poem of grieving and consolation in the tragedy of Covid

This spring and the last,
Death came to our door,
Uninvited—
When I went to answer the door,
Quite unaware of the intruder,
He said:
I am the angel of death;
He was dark, sullen, and fierce,
Nomadic and relentless,
Dressed in black metal,
Feathers and horns,
We refused to let him in.

He broke the walls,
Of our house,
With a savage force,
And left us grieving;
He mistakenly thought,
He had looted us,
Taken away all we had,
And left a gaping hole behind;
Death at least in poetry,
Has never been emptiness,
It is always about presence,
In some form or the other.
Elizabeth Jane Howard,

Shows our loved ones,
Shutting a door or gate,
Behind them,
And disappearing,
Is not dying;
For they always live,
On that periphery,
At the last moment,
Or that beautiful convergence,
On which all of life rests,
Like an awesome dream.

Gabriela Mistral whispers,
In her Spanish poem—
Canto que Amabas
(The Song you Loved),
Yo canto lo que tu amabas, vida mía
Por si te acercas y escuchas, vida mía
Por si te acuerdas del mundo que viviste
Al atardecer yo canto, sombra mía
(I sing what you loved, my life
In case you come closer and listen my dear
In case you remember the world you lived in
At sunset I sing, my shadow).

Death is not emptiness,
But a sea of separation,
Ghada Al Samman,
In her Arabic poem "The Eraser",
Writes out the agony,
Of grieving and separation;
I spend the night writing you love letters,
Then spend my day,
Erasing each—
Word by word.

Your eyes are my golden compasses,
They point me toward,
The sea of separation;
Death—
That fierce unyielding nomad,
Could wrench away,
Only bodies but not hearts,
For the sea of separation,
Can always be crossed,
At any time of the day or night,
All one needs is faith.

Even Saquib Lakhnavi,
The poet and teller of tales,
Had to pause—
Midst all his weavings,
Yearnings and wisdom,
Zamana bade shauq se sun raha tha
Hamin so gaye dastan kahte kahte
(The world was listening intently
I myself fell asleep while telling the tale).

What is death but a road,
To follow those who've gone ahead;
The sea of separation too,
Is filled with oars and wings,
And a golden sun.

Dreaming

Alone—
I watch the white paper boat,
Beginning to sink,
Under the pelting rain,
Its lettering in flowing ink,
Was once,
A poem;
"The husband's message"
Now melting in torrents,
Still shows—
"The oaths you swore
So long ago together."

Once in all its whiteness,
When the two lived together,
It floated—
Glistening,
Gleaming,
Along the little stream,
Near the house where they lived,
Now no more a letter or poems,
Its paper turning soggy,
With harsh tears;
It begins to sink,
Misshapen and crumpled,
Into the rushing tide,
Till it becomes a mood,
In some tired mind.

Lost Wings

Who am I?
Did I ever catch a butterfly?
Me—the butterfly chaser,
Fell into a pit,
And her net was broken.
Whose face is that—
Shadowed in butterfly wings?
But colorless,
With gaps for eyes,
Whose image—
Does the mirror show?
Is it human?
Is it a butterfly?
Does it need attention?
Does it have a soul?
Is it the butterfly catcher again?
Ready with a net and keen eyes,
Whom,
Some butterfly in disguise,
Cursed forever.
Now,
The image is not of anyone I know,
Accursed,
Isolated,
A Wife— butterfly-like
Is looking,
For a lost pair of wings.

Another Planet: Cancer

They stand away,
In an unreal world of dreams,
But I in my real world,
Of impending disaster,
Where Cancer—
Ticks like a time bomb.

She came to Delhi,
All the way from America,
Only for the evening,
To attend a wedding,
She used to be—
My best friend.

Now my best friend,
Is also far away,
Into her world,
Of possibilities,
Expectations,
And pride in achievements.

Now I am also far away,
Tongue-tied;
How do I talk about Cancer?
I am used to telling lies,
And disguising my state,
In silence.

And yes,
Its not me,
That Cancer has got,
Its not me,
Who drifts off with chemotherapy;
Though in heart and soul,
I suffer too,
A strange predicament,
Of not knowing,
What lies ahead.

My mind has become,
A haunted place—
Little holes and gaps,
Break the smug road
Of routine and complacency,
All is not what it seems,
Something gleams,
But I am wary of hope.

Doctors have a way
Of serving prognosis,
Like a slice of cake;
We understand nothing,
Because we are the plates,
On which reality lies.
Surgeries and radiation,
Remove the Cancer,
But how does one heal,
the trauma of Cancer,
In old peaceful ways?

Questionings

Where?
Where has love gone?
Seems it sank like the sun;
Setting below—
Horizons,
Houses,
Streets,
Dogs,
Kids.

Where?
Where has love gone?
When night descends,
Countless faces,
A million stars,
Gleaming in dew,
The moon radiant,
Standing silent and whole,
Gives no reply.

Where?
Where has love gone?
And then,
Midst
Moonbeams,
Lamplights,
Owl hootings,

Slow chirping crickets,
The pall of sleep,
Veils all consciousness.

Where?
Where has love gone?
The thinking must change,
The questions must change,
No more a seeker am I,
Its my business,
To answer all such questions,
To give answers,
Not to perish in pursuit,
But to grow rich with love.

Hypnos

Hypnos—
Cast thy spell!
Over our boat,
Sailing the river of dreams;
So affordable,
No ego,
No fighting,
Along the Lemosyne,
You can be,
Whomever you want,
Love whomever you choose,
And time is unchartered.

You cannot consciously ride,
To a past or future—
Yet here in dreams,
In a moonlit arena,
Bustling with life,
Live subliminal joys.
And forbidden loves,
Hate has no place.

In this gathering,
Only friends collect,
Here is the true life—
In the basement,
Of gnarled, forgotten roots,

That water flowers above,
Is the truth of all desire,
What appears real,
Is merely shadow;
And dreaming,
Is the true state,
Of bliss.

Before the Earth is gone

The night is drowned in silence,
No more the sound of guests;
The only sound—
Is of our breathing,
The only sensation—
Of our beating hearts;
Don't stay away too long,
Or else the earth,
Might shift its orbit.

There is the perfume,
Of freshly bloomed roses,
And no thorn of doubt,
Should break our reverie;
Don't stay away too long,
For the ice caps may melt,
And the sun might swallow us.

Tonight,
The air is filled with promise,
With the ecstasy of waiting,
There is a loss of hunger,
A loss of every sense,
Except the fear of dissolution;
Don't stay away too long,
Otherwise some fingers,
Somewhere may press the button

And the world will end.

This statue of clay,
Has lost its colors,
Its eyes are dimming out,
But still—
Passersby find it pretty,
They stop to look at it,
But nothing lasts forever,
Not mud or stones or clay,
And they keep building,
Monuments, museums, palaces;
Who can build monuments,
That can stand the test of time,
Don't stay away too long.
For when the wind rises,
Even pillars need to move.

Cosmic Love Song

Take the pieces,
Of this graveled heart,
Its million crystals of galaxies,
In your hands;
Put them together,
With a bang, a tremor,
An invocation,
Or a ray of light;
Ask no questions,
As how,
The cosmic heart collapsed,
Leaving only dark matter;
Do not count the missing pieces,
As the cosmic dust,
Slips through your fingers,
Holding loose clay and pebbles,
That are such eternal misfits,
But your boundless kindness,
Will shape a heart again,
Shining like a full moon,
In dreams on the darkest of nights;
The grains hear your footsteps,
And with a quake revive.

The Multi Tasker

Wife—
Shadow,
Seamstress,
Mender,
Darner,
Smoother of sheets,
Stain remover,
Knotter of loose threads,
Weaver of matching shreds,
Unintelligent ponderer of books,
For the sake of cleaning dust,
Silent collector of degrees,
Marker on old calendars,
With pencils and oil stains,
Always disguising the tears,
Always chipping her nails,
In tight buttonholes,
Always putting flowers,
To hide inglorious thoughts,
Never becoming a rose,
That decks lovely hair,
Of models with flowers,
Dyed hair and mascara lashes,
Because of messy fingers.
One day—
Her moment of recompense,

They gave her,
Undue praise and accolades,
That made her husband
Turn to glance at her,
With less than a smile;
That Shadow,
That Seamstress,
That Mender,
That Darner,
That Smoother of sheets,
That Stain remover,
That Knotter of loose threads,
That Weaver of matching shreds,
Unintelligent ponderer of books,
For the sake of cleaning dust—
Looked back,
With half a smile.

The Housewife's Escape

Why did she go—
Without a moment's thought,
Of fleeting joys,
Of daughter's butterfly strokes,
Of son's cycles of returns.

Why did she decide
To leave?
When did it happen?
When was the moment?
That the cat,
Became too heavy,
Perching on her shoulder,
And the parrot's chatter
Became a dither,
A mockery!
An irony!
An unsurmountable grief!
Did Death do her part?
Never to be one again!
What moment is it,
When a wife
Decides to be a woman?
And her heart breaks,
And regenerates,
Into a wild bird,
That no one can snare,

Or tame or overcome;
When did she start out,
On the unholy road,
To herself?

Rules for Girls!

Women and girls,
Are forbidden many things,
They need to play clean,
And not let the mud,
Dirty their dresses;
They need to focus,
Their heart and minds,
Stay obedient,
And grateful.

Once in a while,
A girl dares desire,
To walk,
An untraveled road,
But she needs to remember,
The rules.

Sometimes,
When the head and heart,
Don't meet,
A girl must learn,
To keep moving.
Along preplanned futures,
With or without shoes,
With or without hope,
Never to upset,

Those sacred plans.
At times the universe itself,
Reflects,
In her heart;
But a girl,
Must learn to ignore,
For all such work,
Is the devil's prompting,
Except—
The dirty dishes,
The endless household chores,
Sometimes a ray of sunlight,
May touch her sodden heart,
But the knell of the kitchen,
The calls to duty,
Must be obeyed;
Sometimes just for a second,
Cinderella's shoe comes alive,
What would she not give,
To hold it forever?
The shell-like shoe,
Gives off rainbow colors,
What if she could keep it,
And write her diary in it.

Hallucinogens

Sharp stones,
Rose thorns,
Stale cake cream,
Dust,
Dust,
Dust,
The blossoming of money,
Bursting paper lotuses,
In unreal Japanese lakes,
Flowing under bridges,
In gardens of conditioning;
We must have eaten,
Like Alice,
Too great a dose,
Of the hallucinogen
Reality!
We become virtual,
Virtually real,
and Virtually unreal,
The mysterious deeps,
Whirlpools, ebbs, cortex,
Bubbling, hissing, seething,
Under our feet,
We want to feel real sand,
And the cool water,
We dig the sand,
Looking for shells

Only lost slippers emerge
And shreds of mines,
And human bodies,
As jetsam and flotsam,
The hallucinogenic worlds,
Too farfetched, too unbelievable;
The mangled hives of reality,
Are the vegetable sellers,
Clogged drains and hearts,
Warped roads and minds.
Down under the earth,
A river flows,
Not *Alph*, the sacred river,
Not the river *Kausar* of paradise,
But a river of the underworld,
Of diabolic acid and poison;
Whoever drinks of it,
Becomes its dark turgid waters,
Which escape,
Into embryonic dreams,
Of hallucinogenic reality,
Stifling the psyche of tomorrow,
Here we stand half awakened,
Not dreamers anymore.

Kusum Didi

I remember,
Your simplicity,
Your generosity,
Your beautiful heart;
Served in a spoon of ghee,
In a handful of sweet curd,
Or in the quickly packed lunch,
At my departure.
You served,
Till your last breath,
And got nothing in return;
So say the rules,
Of private schools.
How is it,
That the one,
Who was Annapurna,
Spent her old age starving.

I have thought of you,
And your love,
That shaped me for life;
If you were alive today,
You wouldn't fit,
In today's heartless mold,
Of modern sensibility!

The House in Aligarh

A white-washed brick house,
Balconies with scented Jasmine,
Surrounded,
By Neem and Eucalyptus,
A small street,
Of mud and stones,
In an old-time world—
Dreams walked on it.

At a little bookshop,
At the corner,
We borrowed fifty paise books,
Peering with an oil lamp.

A path unhurried,
And green on either side,
Flower sellers everywhere.
Evening fell with such,
Contemplated silence,
And the balloon seller,
Let loose colored bubbles.

Eid charmed her way,
In *Ghararas* and shiny slippers,
With the jingle of bangles,
Aromas filled the air—
Yakhni pulao, *Biryani*,

Kebabs and *Sheer*,
Wearing their aromas,
In braids with ribbons,
And embroidered kurtas,
Children danced all the way,
To the Idgah.

Mending to the kitchen,
With its grinding stone,
And *burada angeethi*,
Overloaded with cooking,
Yet the loads lightened,
With crackling kurtas,
and the coy touch,
Of simmering silk *Ghararas*.
Memory bolts away,
Like a sleepy cat,
From the old cane chair,
Lying in the soft sunlight.

Aligarh—
Raised its head,
Above the myriad newspapers;
Spilled with the ink of agony,
And the grime of elections,
Wiping itself clean off the flowers,
Off *Ghararas*, *Biryanis*, and *Sheers*,
Hastily blowing out blackened lamps;
Excitement came raging,
In newborn malls,
Car lights flashing,
Brightening gates of flats.

Moonlight stopped singing,
And greeting Chand Raat,

The night before Eid,
Or Ramzan's glittering close.
No one wears clothes,
That dry slowly in the sun,
No one stirs faith,
In huge pots overnight.
No one sits blowing,
A smoky fire,
Or hungers for—
Glassy,
Transparent,
Mornings.

Aligarh—
Just burrowed itself,
In a mobile,
That rings to death,
In the traffic jam,
Across the railway line;
Loudspeakers—
In pompous songs,
Sing of love,
And matrimony,
Signifying only voids.
Near the shrine,
Of Barchi Baba,
Crowds,
Hang their hopes,
And dreams by,
Pink threads and scarves,
And netherworld,
Saunters glumly now,
Only on Thursdays.

Once the British,
Attempted to bury,
The shrine,
Under a railway track;
Each night,
The track would disappear.

Aligarh—
Now peeps,
From behind,
Thin pricked fingers,
That embroider and weep,
At the glamour of Amir Nishan's
Fine garments.

Lunch and ice creams,
Midst the noise of youth,
At crowded Bobby's
And outside,
The begging bowls,
Wait—
For an empty ice cream cone.

Along the crowded lane,
Every day I see,
The old fading face of Aligarh,
Walking unsteadily,
And white-haired,
In between the cars,
That doesn't want to stop,
But they pause,
With disbelief,
To let an old man pass,
Who knows nothing,
About Volkswagen,

Or KFC,
Or Pizza Hut,
Or anything worth knowing;
In his hand,
He holds a time-worn
Alarm clock,
That stopped working long ago.

The Dead Dog

Amidst loud morning chirps,
Wind whistling and whirling,
Warm sunshine over his fur,
The dog curled up was dead;
He was a lone soul,
Who befriended the cars,
And indifferent neighbors,
Who never forgot humanity,
But let a dog wail to death,
On their doorstep;
A dog died last night,
Unsung hero of the night,
Whose pattering footsteps,
Kept the road alive,
And vandals at bay,
Now the street cur,
Is no more;
Who bowed before those,
That gave him blows,
Who loved those,
That shooed him away,
Who survived gratefully,
On leftover scraps,
And who'd wait,
Sitting all evening,
By our gate,
For those golden scraps;

For him, they were more,
Than just food,
They were—
Manna dew,
Straight from heaven.

The Striped Wanderer

Wanderer, Seeker, Mourner—
For a lost green canopy!
Gray-colored squiggle,
Flimsy-tailed squirrel,
Who set up a jittery clamor,
When the tree trembled,
And bent double with an ache,
On the littered earth,
And your bowers,
Toppled many secrets;
You ran hither and thither,
On the twisted electric cable,
My heart beating to your call,
Though words were,
Only a stare of loss and confusion,
In my hand, a piece of bread,
To resolve your dread,
Confusions and restless detours;
But I'll never know what prompts you,
What colors your dreams or hopes,
As you tripped towards me,
A sudden electric thought,
Made you retreat;
Maybe a lapse of communication,
Or was I prodding your fears,
With sharp-axed curiosity,
Or the tree bridging our worlds,

Collapsed into sad, seeping silence;
You have since,
Decided our boundaries,
As unreachable, impenetrable—
And left me standing,
With a piece of bread in hand,
And a gentle sorrow in heart.

Pulsations

Pulsations from far away,
Catch my attention,
And through my script,
Write out their path,
Across worlds of weary light years,
A kindness pulses through,
Like a lamp,
Like a torch,
Like a soft tune,
And then, you know,
That no one is ever alone,
In the vast limitless universe,
Stars, planets, comets,
Have a language,
Without a tongue or pen,
It is the language of love,
That travels like the sunlight,
Bringing rainbows and rain,
Bringing color and fragrance,
Bringing seasons and silences,

Pulsations from far away,
In the blooming flowers,
In the songs of birds,
In the eyes of animals,
In the barks of trees,
Long lessons for humanity,

To cultivate hearing and sight,
To read,
The winds and storms,
To know that moods,
Are both inner and outer,
And each connected,
One day we will learn surely,
Not to enslave beauty,
But to live in its heart;
Not to harvest everything,
But to become part of the harvest;
One day—
We must learn the codes,
That connects us,
To our friends,
In the universe.

Eliot's Nameless Cat

A cat could be,
Augustus,
Bailey,
Plato,
Munkustrap—
Whatever the name,
Cats can make one laugh,
Or shed the concealed tear;
To outcastes of love,
Who even fear shadows,
Cats teach belief;
With the silken whisker,
And perpendicular tail of truce,
They undo bitter discord,
Willing the suspension of disbelief;
For Eliot's cat—
Ineffable,
In a bowl of milk,
Lie all ecstasies,
To soothe away cramps,
And when he chooses slumber,
Over useless gnawing of bones,
Twitching and dreaming,
His ears flutter with names,
Coming through easily enough,
Exploring old dreams,
Learning to give up,

What slips away;
Cat-like eyes glow in the dark,
At dusk licking bruised fur,
Sniffing the air of waiting,
Unpolluted by ticking clocks,
Using armchairs, cushions,
computers and shelves,
To ease out their
tribulations.
Slipping out into the sun,
Chasing shadows,
Quietly admitting defeat,
Smelling the flowers,
Chewing them gently,
With such feline graces
A cat finds a name,
A deep and inscrutable single name.

Koel

When the Koel,
That homeless tramp,
Who slept all winter,
Trilled hope,
On the wire of dawn,
You called to her,
And she gave a reply;
She wasn't seeking you,
My friend,
But her lost soul;
In the mirror of nature,
Restless in spring,
She would sing,
Inspiration to music maestros.

A nomad of seasons,
Her young ones,
Raised in foster nests,
She would call unfatigued,
To that unseen self,
Who whispered in her head,
She heard the stirrings in the leaves,
Of one who never showed himself.

She called all summer long,
For the one,
In the gardens,

In the mango groves,
In the trees;
But alas! For her soul seeking—
Someone just cut,
Her green bowers.

Remembrance

How does one
Embalm,
Snapshots from time,
In one's yellowing album?
How does one
Leave nothing out,
Let nothing die,
Let nothing sink,
Into the Lethe of forgetfulness?
How does one retrace,
Lost pages of school copies,
Torn and soaked in rain?
How does one draw eyes,
With a toddler's fetal mindset,
And fill them again with rainbows?

How does one hold back a sigh?
To see albums covered with dust,
Or aged avatars in Google photos,
And feel the throbbing heart,
Displayed underneath each,
In all its smallness and grandeur,
And all its veins,
With their twists and curves,
Bursting with emotion.

How does one recapture,
All the old colors,
Which like butterflies,
Alight in the mind for seconds,
And never again repeat
Themselves.
Only sometimes,
In memory's map,
Someone speaks,
With such fierce conviction,
That one's life,
Changes forever.

Najma Apa's Birthday

The slow pick-up
Of the car,
Against the morning wind;
And young cyclists,
Rushing to school,
Crossing unopened shops,
And the enclosures,
For *Swachh Bharat*;
The rumble of tractors,
The roar of truck engines,
The rickety passage,
Of unruly three-wheelers,
Ah, Morning, what chaos is this!
Who are they who wake,
And shake their vehicles,
To plow through the roads,
Of concrete not mud;
Yet muddy or slushy,
I drive through the vortex.

And amidst it all,
I remember your soft face,
Over the birthday cake,
Trying to slice layers of memory,
As we continue to grope,
Through traffic lights,
Looking for destination,

Feet heavy on the brakes,
Loud horns blare,
The traffic is jammed.

And again your lighted eyes,
The round white kettle,
White teacups,
As we sit to tea,
And eat your birthday cake,
For many years to come.

Reaching Out

We long to reach out,
And touch mirrors,
Reflecting yesterday's light,
Our fingers caress cracked glass,
That still bears emotions.
Has hand prints and lipstick.

We want to reach out,
And see the sun,
Falling on the glass,
From in between the trees,
And baking terraces;
We want to hold,
The shards of glass,
As the prisms,
And make mockery,
Of today.

Shadow like we withdraw,
Our bodies,
Mere collections of—
Sand, glass, silica, sodium,
Which like dew,
Hold a thousand mansions of light.

Winter Night

That night—
The last star broke,
With a cold anguished sigh,
The clouds scurried by,
Fog wind and chill,
Kept their winter vigil,
The flowers, stone-like,
In their frozen footsteps,
Trees stood specter still,
Grass looked white;
Surely, I thought,
There must be someone,
Beyond all that,
Watching you,
As you passed through the darkness,
Holding my hand.
Not a sound,
Not a footstep,
Nothing broke the dread,
Of that night;
Nature still weeps,
As of that night,
When she lost her poet,
Now that you are gone,
My father,
My friend,
My mentor—

Winter still ponders,
In all its gloominess,
Awaiting your *nostos*,
With deep assurance,
I know—
The flowers of verse,
That you sowed,
Will spring up again,
And dance like daffodils,
Under some wandering cloud.

Banana Tree

Romantic nature
Is nowhere to be found,
Not even with my golden friend—
His huge flapping wings,
Glowing in the sunlight,
Combing out the breeze;
From where does he come?
Whence his knotted roots?
I see him in my dreams,
The dreams of entire humanity;
Banana trees waving placidly,
Hands and fingers mellow green,
Against a brown living earth,
They found this yellow sweetness,
Life-sustaining and scrolled with rice,
Web pages of stories and dainty mats,
Nameless deities carved on them,
Their holy scripts,
This cursed wretch,
I see today—
Is a friend turned, enemy!
A maligned intruder!
A billion-dollar gamble!
A fake health food!
A Dracula or denizen,
Feeding on the blood,
Of his human friends!

Seeking

I look for you,
High and low,
Within and without,
Hopelessly imploring a few words,
But you maintain your silence;
I evaluate your silence,
To mystic proportions,
Singing songs,
Of timeless love,
You remain,
In my heart,
But my eyes cannot see you;
Your words inaudible to my ears,
But my heart can hear you,
What are you?
A fragrance or a song?
I cannot even question,
For fear that I might offend you,
And you might take even,
Your gift of silence away from me,
Only sometimes in dreams,
I perceive your real form,
Like the singing of the pines,
In the hills,
Or the smell of earth,
After the first rainfall.

www.ingramcontent.com/pod-product-compliance
Lightning Source LLC
LaVergne TN
LVHW091031150826
845672LV00006BA/1767

* 9 7 8 9 3 9 1 4 3 1 7 9 2 *